A to Z France

BY JUSTINE AND RON FONTES

children's press®

A Division of Scholastic Inc.
New York Toronto London Auckland Sydney
Mexico City New Delhi Hong Kong
Danbury, Connecticut

Consultant: Adriana Dominguez
Series Design: Marie O'Neill
Photo Research: Candlepants Incorporated

The photos on the cover show the Eiffel Tower (right), a gargoyle from Notre Dame Cathedral (bottom), a French child holding baguettes (center), and a bunch of green grapes (left).

Photographs© 2003: AllSport USA/Getty Images/Alex Livesey: 22; Art Resource, NY/Giraudon: 13 left; Corbis Images: 35 bottom right (Paul Almasy), 13 right (Archivo Iconografico, S.A.), 14 top (Wild Poppies, by Claude Monet, 1873. Archivo Iconografico, S.A./(c) 2003 Artists Rights Society (ARS), New York/ADAGP, Paris), 14 bottom, 15 bottom (Bettmann), 16 top (Anna Clopet), 10 left, 26 top, 36 bottom, 37 right (Owen Franken), 33 top right (Gianni Dagli Orti), 27 right (Marc Garanger), 12 bottom (Antoine Gyori), 4 bottom, 5 top right (Chris Hellier), 5 left (Kit Houghton), 24 left (Catherine Karnow), 37 top left (Charles & Josette Lenars), 36 top (Chris Lisle), 7 (Robert Matheson), 5 bottom right (Naturfoto Honal), 18, 19 (Bryan F. Peterson), 9 left (Photo B.D.V.), 23 right, 28 bottom, 35 top right (Reuters NewMedia Inc.), 4 top (Jeffrey L. Rotman), 34 (Vince Streano), 23 left (TempSport), 12 top (Peter Turnley), cover bottom (Ruggero Vanni), 27 left (Sandro Vannini), 33 bottom left (O. Alamany & E. Vicens), 35 left; Corbis Sygma: 28 top (Olivia Baumgartner), 33 top left (Pascal Parrot), 16 bottom, 32 (Pierre Vauthey); Envision Stock Photography Inc.: 10 right (Curzon Studio), 38 bottom, 38 top (Steven Mark Needham), 11 (Amy Reichman); ImageState: cover top right (Mike Howell), 6 bottom (Brian Lawrence); National Geographic Image Collection: 33 bottom right (Sisse Brimberg), 25 bottom right (Bruce Dale); Nik Wheeler: 8 bottom, 12 right, 17 left; PhotoDisc/Getty Images: 24 top right, 25 top right, 25 left (Martial Colomb), 17 right (Ryan McVay), 29 (PhotoLink), cover center (Nicola Sutton/Life File); PictureQuest/Image Source/elektraVision: cover top left; Stone/Getty Images: 31 (Oliver Benn), 24 bottom right (Michael Busselle), 8 top (Nicholas DeVore), 26 bottom (Steven Rothfeld); Taxi/Getty Images: 6 top (David Noton), 9 bottom right (Stephen Simpson); The Image Bank/Getty Images: 30 (Lionel Isy-Schwart), 9 top right (Yellow Dog Productions); The Image Works/ Yashiro Haga: 37 bottom left.

Map by XNR Productions

Library of Congress Cataloging-in-Publication Data

Fontes, Justine.
  France / by Justine and Ron Fontes.
     p. cm. – (A to Z)
Includes bibliographical references and index.
Contents: Animals – Buildings – Cities – Dress – Exports – Food –
Government – History – Important people – Jobs – Keepsakes – Land
– Map – Nation – Only in France – People – Question – Religion –
School & sports – Transportation – Unusual places – Visiting the
country – Window to the past – X-tra special things – Yearly
festivals – Z – Let's explore more – Meet the authors – Words you know.
  ISBN 0-516-24557-0 (lib. bdg.)   0-516-26808-2 (pbk.)
  1. France–Juvenile literature. [1. France.] I. Title: A to Z France.
II. Fontes, Ron. III. Title. IV. Series.
  DC17.F635 2003
  944 – dc21
                                    2003005836

▪ Contents

A sea urchin's mouth has five jaws.

Animals

Vultures eat animals that are already dead.

Centuries of farming have had a great impact on France's native wildlife. Today, the country has more chickens, cows, pigs, and sheep than wild animals. Many wild animals are protected by France's national parks.

Carmague

Nutria look like giant rats. They are raised for their soft fur.

Flamingos

Small wild horses live in the cold saltwater **marshes** of Southern France. Cowboys use these horses, called Carmagues, to herd the local black bulls.

Big flocks of flamingos also live in France. They live in the lakes of France's **nature preserves**. Young flamingos are grayish brown. They turn pink when they grow up.

Many amazing castles were built along the Loire River.

Buildings

The Louvre Museum has a 71-foot (22 m)-high steel and glass pyramid that was added to it in 1989 by the Chinese-American architect I.M. Pei.

The first "buildings" in France were prehistoric caves. Later, **Celtic** tribes built stone tombs. The Ancient Romans came and built theaters, baths, and **aqueducts**.

Paris

Cities

Paris is one of the most beautiful cities in the world. It is the capital of France and the nation's largest city. It was founded by the Romans.

Paris has one of the world's largest art museums. Many artists and writers have created their best works in Paris. The Louvre Museum has many famous paintings, including Leonardo da Vinci's *Mona Lisa*.

In Brittany, folk costumes for women and girls include lace trimmed bonnets.

Dress

Since the 17th Century, Paris has been the fashion capital of the world. The French take pride in dressing with flair. A silk scarf or a hat can turn an outfit into a work of art.

France is famous for high-fashion.

Chic

(sheeq)
means stylish.

Vogue

(vohg)
means fashion.

Each region has its own special style of dress. Many young city people wear jeans, sneakers, and T-shirts. People who live in the countryside, wear folk costumes on holidays.

These grapes will be made into wine.

Exports

The French have made wine since they were part of the Roman Empire. The country is famous for producing the finest wines in the world. Wine is named after the region where it is made.

France exports about 500 different kinds of cheese! Like wine, cheeses are named after the places where they are made.

France is also famous for its perfumes. Huge fields of flowers in Southern France are **harvested** to make perfume. France also exports electronic equipment, cars, trains, machines, chemicals, and movies.

French Toast Recipe

WHAT YOU NEED:

- 2 eggs
- 1 cup milk
- 1 teaspoon vanilla
- a pinch of salt
- about half a stale baguette (8-10 slices cut about 1 inch thick)
- butter
- honey, syrup, or powdered sugar

HOW TO MAKE IT:

Beat the first four ingredients together in a shallow container. Dip bread on one side, then turn to soak the other. Cover and let bread soak in egg mixture for an hour, or in the refrigerator overnight. Melt butter in a big skillet over medium heat. Cook bread till golden brown, about 3-5 minutes on each side. Serve with your favorite sweetener.

Food

To the French, cooking is an art, and every meal is a joy. *Baguettes*, which are long, thin, crusty breads, are served with most French meals. Baguettes get stale fast and French cooks hate to waste food. So, they came up with a delicious way to enjoy it. Ask an adult to help you make some French Toast using the recipe above.

11

Before he became the current president of France, Jacques Chirac was the mayor of Paris.

The French Parliament

Government

In 1991, Edith Cresson became the first female prime minister of France.

French people 18 or older can vote. Every five years they elect a new president. The president appoints a prime minister. The president deals with other countries. The prime minister oversees the government within France.

The storming of the Bastille on July 14, 1789, started the French Revolution. The Bastille was a prison for people who went against the king and queen.

Joan of Arc claimed to hear the voice of God and led the French army to victory.

History

In ancient times, Celtic people named Gauls lived in France. In 52 B.C. Julius Caesar's Roman army defeated the Gauls. The Romans brought roads, cities, law, and winemaking to France.

In the 5th Century A.D., France was taken over by the Franks. In time, France became the most powerful country in Europe. In 1337, England and France began a series of battles that lasted over 100 years. This was called the Hundred Years' War.

France was ruled by many kings until the **French Revolution**. Then, in 1789, the poor people of France revolted against their rich rulers. France became a **democracy**.

Poppies by Claude Monet, 1873

Important People

Many of the world's greatest painters studied or lived in France. Several art movements started there. An art movement is a style of art.

Claude Monet

Henri Matisse loved painting with bright colors.

Impressionism was one art movement. Impressionists used paint to explore light and shadow. The movement got its name from a painting by Claude Monet called *Impression, Sunrise.*

Monet loved to paint flowers. He often painted outside. He painted the same things at different times of the day to show the effect of sunlight on color.

Henri Matisse was another great artist. He was a law clerk until he got very sick. While he was getting better, Matisse started painting. He quit law and became a leader of the modern art movement.

Experts test perfumes. They are known as "noses."

Jobs

Seven out of ten French people have service jobs. That means that they work in schools, hospitals, banks, offices, restaurants, or stores. Some work in factories too.

Many French people work on small farms. They raise cows and other animals or crops.

French workers get 5 weeks vacation every year. In the summer, many go to the beaches or the mountains.

Cooks from all over the world come to France to become great chefs.

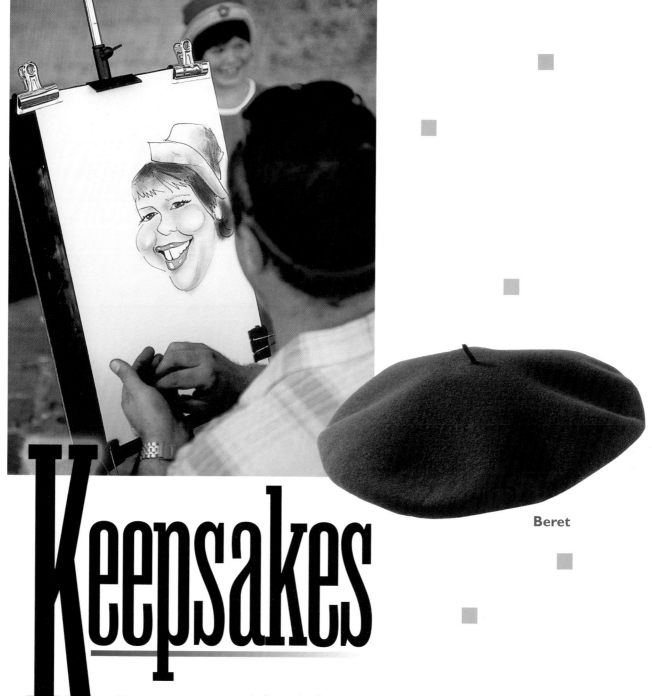

Beret

Keepsakes

Berets are round, flat cloth caps worn by many French people. They are practical and stylish.

Many artists wear berets to keep warm while they are drawing outside. France is full of street artists. Some will draw your picture in just a few minutes. This can make an excellent **souvenir.** The English word *souvenir* comes from the French verb souvenir, which means "to remember."

These fields of lavender will be harvested to make perfume.

Land

France is the third largest country in Europe. It has fertile soil and a comfortable climate.

The French Alps

France has everything from snow-capped mountains to Mediterranean beaches. It has thick forests and many miles of good farmland.

The country also includes islands in the Caribbean, Indian, and Pacific Oceans. Corsica is a big island in the Mediterranean Sea near Italy that is also part of France. The famous Seine River runs through Paris.

Île

(eel)
means island.

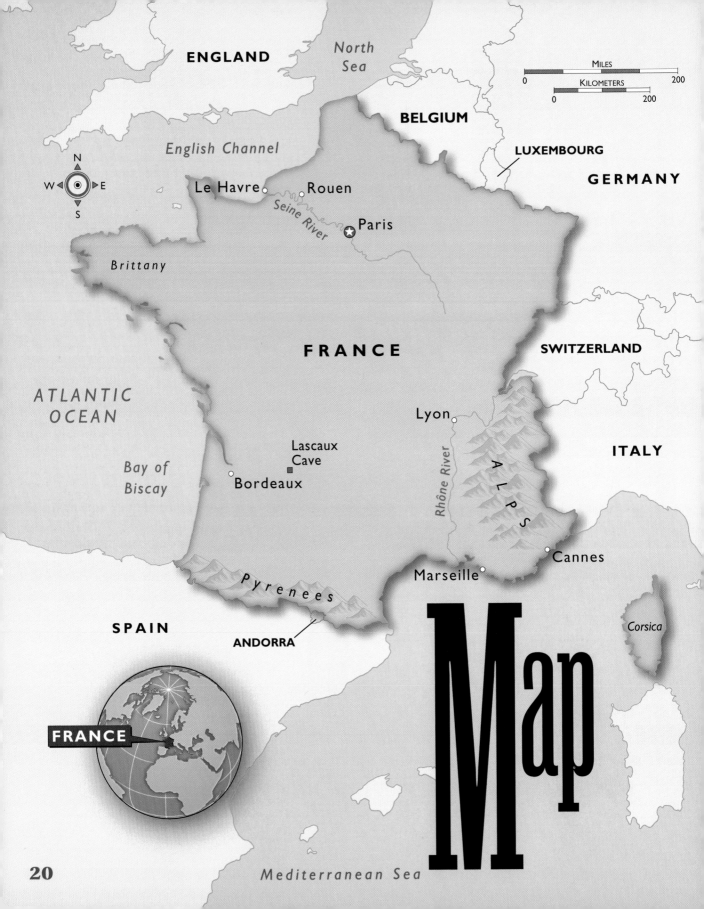

ENGLAND

North Sea

BELGIUM

LUXEMBOURG

GERMANY

English Channel

N
W · E
S

Le Havre   Rouen

Seine River

Paris

Brittany

FRANCE

SWITZERLAND

ATLANTIC OCEAN

Lyon

Rhône River

ITALY

A L P S

Lascaux Cave

Bay of Biscay

Bordeaux

Cannes

Marseille

Pyrenees

SPAIN

ANDORRA

Corsica

Map

FRANCE

20

Mediterranean Sea

MILES
0   200
KILOMETERS
0   200

Nation

The current French flag dates back to the French Revolution in 1789. Saint Martin, a rich soldier, cut his blue coat in half to share with a cold beggar. Blue stands for the duty of rich people to help the poor. Joan of Arc helped drive the English out of France. White stands for Joan of Arc and the Virgin Mary. White later became the color of French royalty, too. Red is the color of Saint Denis, the patron saint of Paris.

Only in France

The most famous bicycle race in the world takes place in France every summer. Thousands of people go to see the Tour de France, and millions watch it on television.

The Tour de France was started in 1903 by Henri Desgranges. He was the owner of a sports newspaper called *Le Velo*.

The Tour de France lasts for about three weeks and covers nearly 2,500 miles (4,023 km)! Riders come from many countries. There are 9 riders on each team. Each rider has a special skill, like sprinting or climbing.

The Tour de France covers a different route every year. Racers ride their bicycles through many different parts of France, including steep mountains such as the Alps and the Pyrenees. The route sometimes includes nearby countries, like Belgium, Germany, or Spain. Riders pedal their hearts out to be the first to cross the finish line.

People

Most French people were born in France. Some were born in former French **colonies**, such as Algeria.

Many French people feel that old buildings have more character than new ones.

Different regions of France have different customs. In the Alsace region, people cook and dress like their German neighbors. However, the French language unites all of the people of France.

About three-quarters of the people in France live in cities.

People in the countryside often live in small houses in villages, or on farms. The houses are usually made of stone and have wooden shutters.

Chateau

(SHA-toh)
means house or castle.

Question

What are truffles?

Truffles are a kind of mushroom that grow underground on the roots of oak and hazelnut trees. These black mushrooms have a fragrant, nutty flavor. French chefs like to use truffles in sauces, omelets, and meat dishes.

Truffles are rare and expensive because people can't grow them on farms. They must be found in the wild. People train pigs and sometimes dogs to sniff for truffles.

Notre Dame Cathedral

Stained glass window showing Bernadette and the Virgin Mary

Religion

Over three-quarters of French people are Roman Catholic. There are also over 3 million Muslims in France. There are Jewish people, Protestants, and a small number of Hindus, Buddhists, and people of other faiths too.

The biggest underground church in the world is at Lourdes. In 1858, a 14-year-old girl named Bernadette claimed to see the Virgin Mary there. After that, she touched the ground and a spring poured out! Many people believe that the water at Lourdes can cure diseases.

School & Sports

French children aged 6 to 16 must go to school. Public schools are free. The Catholic Church runs most of the private schools. College is free for students who pass a tough test. Over 99 percent of French adults can read and write.

The French also enjoy playing sports. They like team sports such as soccer, baseball, and volleyball. They also ride horses and bicycles and go jogging, skating, skiing, and hiking.

This car runs on electricity!

Transportation

France has excellent highways. Two long highway tunnels connect France and Italy. The Chunnel is a railroad tunnel that runs under the English Channel to connect France and Great Britain.

France has the fastest passenger trains in the world. TGV stands for "train à grande vitesse," which means high-speed train. TGVs can go up to 186 miles (299 km) per hour!

People also travel by bus, subway, ship, moped, bicycle, and airplane. Air France is one of the world's biggest airlines.

Unusual Places

Mont-Saint-Michel is a rocky **islet** in the northwestern part of France. The region is known for its tides. You can walk across the sand when the tide is out. But, watch out! When the tide comes in, Mont-Saint-Michel becomes an island.

The Abbey at Mont-Saint-Michel is known as "The Marvel." An abbey is a building where **monks** or nuns live. This **medieval** abbey was built on top of a granite peak surrounded by a fort.

Visiting the Country

People who can afford to go anywhere often choose to visit the **Côte d'Azur**. It has many beautiful beaches, as well as art galleries, museums, and fine restaurants. The area gets its name from the dazzling blue of the sky and water, which attracts many artists.

The most famous cave in France is at Lascaux. The Hall of Bulls is inside.

Window to the Past

Caves in France shelter paintings made by Cro-Magnons, the ancient **ancestors** of modern people. The animals they painted were hunted about 20,000 years ago.

Cro-Magnons used clay, minerals, and burned bones to create yellow, brown, red, and black paints.

In 1940, four boys looking for a lost dog found a cave decorated with ancient art. Since then, several other caves filled with paintings have been found in Southern France.

Cro-Magnon people lived in caves and hunted with weapons made out of bone and stone. Scientists believe the paintings might have been part of a magic ritual asking for help in the hunt.

Many of the kinds of animals they painted still live in France today.

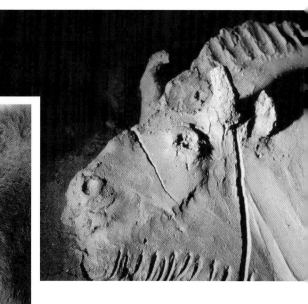

Twelve streets meet under the enormous Arc de Triomphe in Paris.

X-tra Special Things

Cannes Film Festival

Wax heads

The Eiffel Tower was built in 1889 in honor of the 100th anniversary of the French Revolution. Gustave- Alexandre Eiffel designed the steel tower, as well as the frame for the Statue of Liberty. The Eiffel Tower weighs 7,000 tons!

During the French Revolution many rich and royal people were beheaded. Wax artist Madame Tussaud searched through piles of **corpses** to find famous heads from which to make masks of the faces of the dead.

France has other types of artists too. The first moviemakers were French. Every year, moviemakers from all over the world come to the International Film Festival in Cannes.

The Lavender Festival in Provence is one of many harvest festivals in France.

Yearly Festivals

Most French holidays are Catholic. Many towns have summer festivals with music, dancing, shows, and parades.

These men are celebrating Bastille Day.

Each February, Menton, the lemon-growing capital of France, holds a Citrus Festival with floats made of fruit.

In Nice, Carnival is celebrated with boat races, fireworks, music, dance, and parades with giant floats.

Since 1435, the city of Orléans honors Joan of Arc with a festival.

The custom of decorating trees for Christmas started in the 16th century in the town of Alsace. On Christmas Eve, French children put out their shoes, instead of stockings, for "le Père Noël," or Santa Claus.

Bastille Day is a national holiday that recalls the start of the French Revolution. Every July 14, the French celebrate their freedom from royal rule with big parades.

Citron

means lemon.

Zeste

Zeste is the colorful, outer peel of an orange, lemon, lime, or other citrus fruit. The zest has a very intense flavor. Grated or peeled off the fruit, zest is often used in baking, candy making, or to add flavor and color to sauces and salad dressings.

Just a sprinkling of zest can mean the difference between plain and pretty—and between ordinary and…French!

French and English Words

ancestor (AN-sess-tur) a family member who lived long ago

aqueduct (A-kwuh-dukt) a structure that carries a large amount of flowing water

beret (buh-RAY) a round, flat cap worn by many French people and artists

Celtic (SEL-tik) the Western European tribes living in England and France before the Romans, or people now living in Ireland, Wales, Scotland, and other places

century (SEN-chuh-ree) a period of 100 years

chateau (sha-TOH) a large, French country house or castle

chic (sheeq) French word for style

colony (KOL-uh-nee) a group of people who leave their country to live in another place

corpses (KORP- sez) the remains or bones of dead people

Côte d'Azur (kawt-du-ZURE) French for Blue Coast, meaning the coast of Southern France famous for its blue skies and waters

democracy (di-MOK-ruh-see) a system of government in which a country's people vote for leaders

French Revolution (french rev-uh-LOO-shuhn) the violent uprising that replaced the King with a democratic government in France in 1789

harvest gathering crops that are ripe

île (eel) French word for island

Impressionism (im-PRESH-uh-niz-uhm) a French art movement concerned with the effect of light on color and mood

islet (EYE-let) a small island

marsh a place where the land is low and wet

medieval (mee-DEE-vuhl) a period in history from about 500 A.D. to 1450

monk (muhngk) A man who has devoted his life to God. Monks live in religious communities

nature preserve a place where animals are protected and can live free

peintre (PEN-treh) French word for painter

revolt (ri-vohlt) a fight against the government or other authority

souvenir (soo-vuh-NIHR) something you keep to remind you of a place or person

vogue (vogh) French word for fashion

Let's Explore More

Look What Came From France by Miles Harvey, Franklin Watts, 1999

A Visit to France by Rob Alcraft, Heinemann Library, 1999

France (Ticket To Series) by Tom Streissguth, Carolrhoda Books, 1997

Websites

www.info-france-usa.org/kids/
Read an interview with the French Ambassador to the United States, learn about French culture, geography, history, language, and play games!

www.travelforkids.com/Funtodo/France/france.htm
See photos of places of interest in Paris, Normandy, Brittany, the Loire Valley, and other parts of France.

www2.ac-toulouse.fr/eco-belbeze-union/us_blt.htm
Learn about France, connect with French school children and French websites.

Index

Meet the Authors

JUSTINE & RON FONTES have written nearly 400 children's books together. Since 1988, they have published *critter news*, a free newsletter that keeps them in touch with publishers from their home in Maine.

The Fonteses have written many biographies and early readers, as well as historical novels and other books combining facts with stories. Their love of animals is expressed in the nature notes columns of *critter news*.

During his childhood in Tennessee, Ron was a member of the Junior Classical League and went on to tutor Latin students. At 16, Ron was drawing a science fiction comic strip for the local newspaper. A professional artist for 30 years, Ron has also been in theater as a costumer, makeup artist, and designer.

Justine was born in New York City and worked in publishing while earning a BA in English Literature Phi Beta Kappa from New York University. Thanks to her parents' love of travel, Justine visited most of Europe as a child, going as far north as Finland. During college, she spent time in France and Spain.